BE HAPPY,

LICK SOMEONE TODAY.
(SLURP, SLURP)

DOG-MAS

DOG—MAS

SIMPLE TRUTHS
FROM A WISE PET
AS REVEALED TO
BILL ZIMMERMAN
AND ILLUSTRATED BY
TOM BLOOM

■ HAZELDEN®

Hazelden

Center City, Minnesota 55012-0176

ISBN: 1-56838-046-1

EDITOR'S NOTE

Hazelden offers a variety of information on chemical
dependency and related areas. Our publications do not
necessarily represent Hazelden's programs, nor do they officially
speak for any Twelve Step organization.

*For my daughter,
Carlota,
who with open heart
found Dynamite
and saved her
life.
And for Dynamite,
who has given
us all only love in
return.*

—BILL ZIMMERMAN

❧ PAW-WORD ❧

My dog, Dynamite, comforts me in the early morning just with her presence. She comes to me to love her, to touch and pet her. I give this willingly, for in comforting her, giving her ballast, I find my own grounding for the day.

My dog has always shown me all the kindness of her nature, never holding back, constant and generous in seeing me through personal losses. Hard as I might try, I could never be as unselfish and kind as she. How privileged I am to know Dynamite.

My little dog has taught me how to have fun, to relax more, and to enjoy the fine weather and new grass. She has shown me what loyalty is. In short, she has helped me become a better human being.

I wrote this book to share with you the wisdom I have

learned from Dynamite. I try to imagine what words she would use, if she could, to impart her simple truths and reveal her DOG-MAS. Follow them and they will show you, as they have me, how to live a better life.

Bill Zimmerman

P.S. You are warmly encouraged to bend the dog ears placed on some of the right-hand pages. Bend an ear to discover a joyful message.

Another Hazelden title by Bill Zimmerman
and illustrated by Tom Bloom . . .

The Little Book of Joy:
An Interactive Journal
for Thoughts, Prayers, and Wishes.

HAZELDEN

1-800-328-0098 (Toll-Free U.S., Canada, and the Virgin Islands)

1-612-257-4010 (Outside the U.S. and Canada)

1-612-257-1331 (24-Hour FAX)

DOGSCENTS

WAYS TO APPROACH LIFE

GO OUT INTO THE WORLD
INQUISITIVELY,
SNIFF, SNIFF
ALL AROUND YOU WITH
PASSION,
THERE ARE SO MANY GOOD
SMELLS,

A »DYNAMITE« THOUGHT

GREET EACH DAY WITH HOPE AND EXPECTATION. WIPE FROM YOUR MEMORY ANY HURT OR SLIGHT FROM THE DAY BEFORE. BY DOING SO, YOU SET A GOOD EXAMPLE FOR YOUR HUMANS.

EVERY PUDDLE IS AN
OPPORTUNITY.
DON'T MISS ANY.

ALWAYS
FIND TIME TO
PLAY.

ARF
ARF!
BEND AN EAR

REMEMBER TO SHARE THE QUIET WITH SOMEONE YOU LOVE.

GET LOTS OF EXERCISE
AND SLEEP,

AND DRINK PLENTY OF
WATER,

SHAKE OFF THE DAY.
NOW STRETCH AND RELAX.

(EVEN ROLL ON THE RUG.)

BARK
BARK!
BEND AN EAR

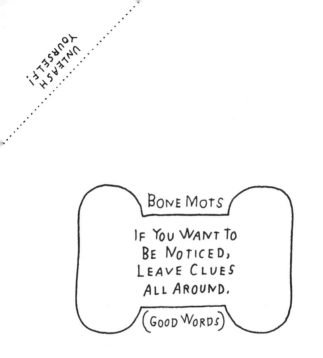

BONE MOTS

IF YOU WANT TO
BE NOTICED,
LEAVE CLUES
ALL AROUND.

(GOOD WORDS)

RUN AFTER A SQUIRREL
OR TWO. YOU DON'T HAVE
TO CATCH ANY, BUT

IT WILL BE FUN
FOR A WHILE.
(PANT, PANT)

A »DYNAMITE« THOUGHT

WHEN YOU GET SOAKED, SHAKE YOURSELF DRY. PREPARE FOR ANOTHER GO ROUND.

STUDY THE HUMANS YOU MEET
BEFORE COMMITTING TO THEM. SNIFF
THEM. TILT YOUR HEAD. BE PATIENT.
THEY WILL COME AROUND IN TIME.

A »DYNAMITE« THOUGHT

KEEP SOME FAVORITE TOYS NEARBY.

YOU NEVER KNOW WHEN YOU'LL
NEED THEM IN A MOMENT OF
UNCERTAINTY OR SADNESS,

ALWAYS BE CURIOUS.
THERE'S SO MUCH TO
SEE AND LEARN.

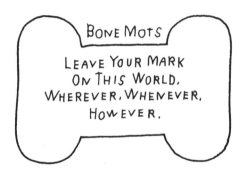

BONE MOTS

LEAVE YOUR MARK
ON THIS WORLD,
WHEREVER, WHENEVER,
HOWEVER.

KNOW WHEN TO RETREAT.
TO DO SO WITH PRIDE
IS STILL A VICTORY.

A »DYNAMITE« THOUGHT

REMEMBER TO
ROLL OVER

AND LOOK AT LIFE
FROM A NEW
PERSPECTIVE.

TAKE LONG WALKS,
THEY ARE GOOD FOR YOU
AND CLEAR THE SOUL.

BONE MOTS

WAG YOUR TAIL.
(EVEN IF YOU DON'T HAVE ONE.)
SHARE YOUR HAPPINESS.
(WIGGLE, WIGGLE)

MAINTAIN A CORE OF
INDEPENDENCE

THIS WILL MAKE
HUMANS RESPECT YOU MORE AND
APPRECIATE YOUR STRONG NATURE.

A »DYNAMITE« THOUGHT

TAKE COMFORT IN YOUR
HEARTH.
IT CAN BE COLD OUTSIDE,
YOU KNOW.

A Bit of Kibble from a Hollywoof Movie Star

BURY YOUR CARES!

BONE MOTS

EAT WHEN
FOOD IS OFFERED.
YOUR NEXT MEAL MAY
NOT COME SO EASILY.

DO A LITTLE DANCE OF JOY
FOR THEM. MAKE THEM SMILE.
ARF, ARF.

ALWAYS KISS THE
HAND THAT FEEDS YOU,

OR AT LEAST GIVE IT A
LICK,

TIPS
ON
LOYALTY
AND
LOVE

A »DYNAMITE« THOUGHT

BE LOYAL TO THOSE
WHO FIRST DISCOVERED AND
NURTURED YOU.
NEVER BETRAY THEM.
IT'S NOT GOOD TO BE FICKLE.

BE LOVING TO
AND PROTECTIVE OF

THOSE WHO ARE KIND
TO YOU.

BE GENTLE AND KIND,

THERE IS ALREADY SO MUCH
PAIN IN OUR WORLD.

RUB UP AGAINST SOMEONE
WHO LOVES YOU.
NUZZLE THEM. (NMMNMM)

BE UNSELFISH
IN YOUR LOVE.
REMEMBER, YOU ARE NOT
THE CAT.

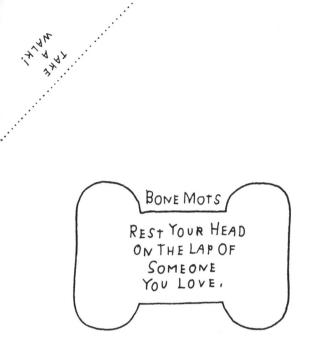

TAKE A WALK!

BONE MOTS

REST YOUR HEAD
ON THE LAP OF
SOMEONE
YOU LOVE.

DON'T BE SAD WHEN THE HUMANS
YOU LOVE LEAVE YOU BEHIND.
THEY WILL RETURN BECAUSE OF
THEIR LOVE, HAVE FAITH IN THEM.

A »DYNAMITE« THOUGHT

TEND TO
THE NEEDS
OF YOUR
HUMAN
WHO COMES
IN WET
FROM THE
RAIN.

A BIT OF KIBBLE FROM A ARFLETIC TRAINER

BEING RESPONSIBLE TO OTHERS
IS A RESPONSIBILITY OF YOURS.

GO FOR IT!

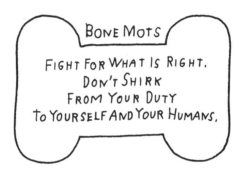

BONE MOTS

FIGHT FOR WHAT IS RIGHT.
DON'T SHIRK
FROM YOUR DUTY
TO YOURSELF AND YOUR HUMANS.

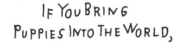

IF YOU BRING
PUPPIES INTO THE WORLD,

BE PREPARED
TO TAKE CARE OF THEM
WHILE THEY GROW UP.

BE AFFECTIONATE,

NEVER BE RESTRAINED IN
YOUR LOVE. (SLURP)

I NEED A NAP!

BE PRACTICAL.

KNOW WHEN TO BARK, WHEN
TO YELP, WHEN TO WHINE, AND
ABOVE ALL, KNOW WHEN TO BE
QUIET.

SOME PRACTICAL POINTERS

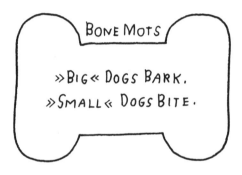

BONE MOTS

»BIG« DOGS BARK.
»SMALL« DOGS BITE.

CULTIVATE YOUR ABILITY TO
FALL ASLEEP AT THE DROP OF A
HAT.

AND NAP, NAP, NAP. ONE CAN
RARELY GET TOO MANY NAPS.

(YAWN)

TAKE TIME TO GROOM
YOURSELF,
KEEP CLEAN,

BE SMART,

LEARN TO SPEAK UP,
WHEN TO BEG, AND EVEN
HOW TO ROLL OVER
AND PLAY DEAD.

YIP!

BEND AN EAR

FIND A FAVORITE SPOT
SOMEWHERE, AND MAKE
IT YOURS.

A »DYNAMITE« THOUGHT

SOMETIMES,
YOU JUST HAVE TO YIP, BARK AND HOWL

TO RID YOUR SOUL OF ITS DEMONS,
BE WILD ONCE IN A WHILE.

A BIT OF KIBBLE FROM A BARKEOLOGIST

BE PRUDENT.

REMEMBER TO BURY SOME BONES
WHERE YOU CAN FIND THEM.
PLAN YOUR FUTURE.

JUMP HURDLES!

BONE MOTS

TALE OF A TAIL

WAG IT IF YOU'RE GLAD,
DRAG IT IF YOU'RE SAD.

FEAR NOT
THE BIG SNEEZE—
IT'S A HEALTHY WAY
TO CLEAR YOUR HEAD.

TROUBLES CAN BE
SHAKEN AWAY, TOO.

A »DYNAMITE« THOUGHT

KNOW WHEN TO BARE
YOUR FANGS AND CLAWS.
DON'T LET OTHERS
ABUSE YOU.

KNOW WHERE YOU'RE
GOING,

BUT BE AWARE OF WHAT'S
FOLLOWING YOU,

BONE MOTS

BE GENTLE WITH
ALL HUMANITY.

DON'T WORRY IF
YOU HAVE DOG BREATH.

IT DOESN'T MEAN YOU'RE
NOT LOVABLE. YOU ARE,
YOU KNOW IT.

A »DYNAMITE« THOUGHT

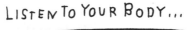

LISTEN TO YOUR BODY...

...AND KNOW ENOUGH
TO LIE DOWN AT THE END
OF A LONG DAY.

MAY YOU LEARN TO SPEAK TO ANIMALS IN THEIR LANGUAGE.

BILL ZIMMERMAN, the creator of *DOG-MAS*, has been a question-er all his life. A journalist for more than twenty years and a prize-win-ning editor, Zimmerman is special projects editor for *Newsday*, one of the nation's largest newspapers. His other books are *The Little Book of Joy: An Interactive Journal for Thoughts, Prayers, and Wishes; How to Tape Instant Oral Biographies*, a book that teaches you how to capture your family stories on audio and video tape; *Make Beliefs*, a magical gift book for the imagina-tion; *Lifelines: A Book of Hope*, which offers comforting thoughts; and *A Book of Questions to Keep Thoughts and Feelings*, a new form of diary/journal.

Dynamite, our wise revealer of simple truths, was discovered in an ASPCA pound by my daughter, Carlota, who wisely saw beauty in the little dog's soul. This sad, frightened-looking pooch, under Carlota's love and care, blossomed into a beautiful, loving, protective pet. She rules our roost, and we love every moment of it.

TOM BLOOM has worked doggedly for a number of years doing drawings in a fetching style. He's paper trained, with work appearing in *The New York Times, Newsday, The New Yorker, Barron's, Fortune, Games* and others. He has received all shots, is good with kids, and has never bitten anyone. Currently, he and his mate board in New York with the pups.

SHARE WITH US

Dear Reader,

Please share with us the simple truths you have learned from your own pet. Perhaps we can incorporate some of them in future editions. We also welcome your comments and suggestions to make *DOG-MAS* funnier and wiser. Please write to: Bill Zimmerman, Guarionex Press, 201 West 77 Street, New York, NY 10024.